The Simple
Baby-Led Weaning
Cookbook #2020

Quick and Healthy Recipes for Babies, Toddlers & the Whole Family incl. Weekly Meal Planner

[1st Edition]

Olivia Newman

Table of Contents

Introduction

As your baby grows, there are several little milestones on her journey to become an independent human to look forward to. Arguably one of the most important ones is the transition from breastfeeding to solid food. A baby's foray into solids opens her up to an exciting new world of textures and flavors. There are plenty of opinions about how this mighty little step should take place. There was a time parents would introduce new food by adding rusk into a baby's bottle along with milk. The traditional approach these days is to serve a baby mushy or pureed peas with a small spoon or fingertip and coax her to open her tiny mouth. However, a growing number of parents are opting to give their babies more control over how and what they put into their mouths. This system of weaning is known as baby-led weaning.

What is baby-led weaning?

Coined by health visitor Gill Rapley in 2003, baby-led weaning is a weaning approach that was made popular in the UK and is gradually gaining traction in the US and other countries. Baby-led weaning is an unstructured and relaxed approach for offering solid food to a baby. This method involves allowing a baby to feed herself with little or no assistance from an adult. Here, the baby is served soft pieces of solid food that are held in the hand instead of being served on a spoon as in the traditional approach. In baby-led weaning manageable bits of family foods, cooked-for-purpose are served on a baby's plate and the baby is allowed to feed herself what she wants at her own pace.

Why baby-led weaning is different

This method essentially bypasses pureed food and transitions straight to solid finger foods. Hence it is used only for baby's who are capable of feeding themselves (6 months of age and above). While baby-led weaning remains a slightly controversial topic among parents, dieticians and health care professionals, most people agree that this approach offers a lot of benefits for babies.

According to the American Academy of Pediatrics and other baby nutrition experts, the best time to begin baby-led weaning is when your baby is about 6 months old. Most babies are already able to sit up by themselves and hold objects by this age. Also, they would have stopped the tongue-thrust reflex which causes them to push substances out of their mouths at this age. A baby's intestines are also well developed to digest solid food at this age.

Benefits and possible future advantages of baby-led weaning

Advocates of baby-led weaning and researchers say that there are plenty of advantages in this feeding approach compared to traditional feeding. These advantages are both in the present and long term as well. Here are some of the benefits and possible future advantages of baby-led weaning:

Allows baby to get familiar with different food flavors and textures: with traditional feeding, babies are fed pureed food or mashed cereals. They are essentially restricted in the variety of food they are exposed to and limited in terms of flavor and texture. Baby-led weaning allows babies to eat from regular family meals prepared specially for a baby's diet. This introduces different food flavors and texture. Experts say an early introduction of various foods like this may lead to the development of healthier food preferences later in life

Dealing with allergies: some studies reveal that trying out a variety of foods at an early age may make it less likely for a baby to develop a food allergy later in life. Even when this is not the case an early introduction to various food types will help parents discover a food strategy early in a baby's life for better management.

Baby will develop better feeding habits: it is believed that bay-led weaning can potentially better and healthier feeding habits in the future. Some studies claim that babies who are weaned through baby-led weaning are less likely to become obese in future compared t babies that are spoon-fed. In traditional spoon-feeding, the parents are in control of feeding. The implication of this is that the baby may be fed too fast and maybe fed wit more than they need causing them to begin to ignore feelings of fullness. In baby-led weaning, your child will determine when she has had enough (just like in breastfeeding). This makes self-regulation based on hunger levels possible. Also, when babies are allowed to eat on their own, they learn to chew their food before swallowing. This is a highly beneficial feeding habit that aids the digestion of food.

Improves hand-eye coordination and dexterity: baby-led weaning will be messy at first. There will be bits and pieces of food dropping and flying around as babies try to navigate feeding on their own. However, with time, the baby will begin to learn and improve hand-eye coordination. Babies that are fed this way are more likely to be dexterous compared to those who had to rely entirely on their parents.

It is Convenient and cheaper: in traditional weaning, parents have to spend time blending cereals and peas for baby, keep the food frozen to preserve and defrost each time they feed them. If you cannot prepare homemade food, you may need to buy jars of baby food formulated specifically for this purpose. But for baby-led weaning, baby feeds on the same food as everyone else in the family with only slight modifications. This is a lot more convenient and easier. Also, although you have to monitor baby as she eats in baby-led weaning, you don't have to spend the entire time feeding her as in traditional weaning.

Rules for introducing baby-led weaning

It is okay to be skeptical about letting your 6-months old bay handle pieces of food on their own. However, you will be amazed at your baby's ability to quickly learn and adapt. If you have decided to go the route of baby-led weaning, here are some basic principles you should keep in mind:

Ensure that your baby is ready: the question of when to introduce baby-led weaning is is a crucial question most parents have about baby-led weaning. Generally, experts say your baby should be 6 months of age or older. However, because the developmental process varies from baby to baby, this age may not be applicable for all. As a general rule, before you allow your baby to feed herself, ensure that she's able to site up in a high chair on her own. Your baby must have also developed good neck strength can move chewed (or gummed food) through her mouth on her own.

Expect a big mess so prepare for it: when you leave a 6-months old baby to feed himself, its okay if its a messy affair. At first, it may only seem that your baby is playing with rather than eating it. Expect some smashing, smearing and outright dropping of the food. As part of your preparation, you should buy a big bib or smock and dress your baby in a diaper. You may want to lay a newspaper or towel on the floor under your baby's high chair.

Continue to breastfeed or bottle-feed alongside: babies get most of the nutrition they need in their early months from breast milk or baby formula designed specifically for that purpose. While introducing solid food is an essential process, make the transition gradual by continuing breastfeeding or bottle-feeding.

Cut foods into thick strips or sticks: While cutting food into tiny bit-sized bits seems like a good idea, it does not work that way. Instead, you should slice the food into thick strips that your baby can hold in her little hands and chew gradually.

Don't rush it: at the beginning, your baby will only need 1 or 2 pieces of food at a time. There's no need to overwhelm her with too many food choices at the beginning. You can start slowly and gradually increase the quantity and variety of food you serve.

Bowls and plates may not work: when you are starting baby-led weaning, you don't need to worry about plates and bowls. Your baby will most likely toss them on the floor while eating. Luckily, most high chairs come with inbuilt trays and you can place the food pieces directly on them. Spoons might not work at first too so feel free to let your baby handle the food with his hands.

Let your baby dine with the family: this is another interesting advantage of the baby-led weaning approach. Eating is a social activity and you will aid your baby's development when your little one can see and mimic you as you eat. Just ensure that what you are serving your little one is baby-appropriate.

Expect some gagging: as your baby tries to maneuver lumps of food in his mouth you should expect some gagging. This is a safe response that should be expected. Many parents panic because they think their baby is choking on the food. Gagging is a safe and normal response and is a lot different from chocking. A chocking child will have a terrifying look, will be unable to breathe and will stay silent. Gagging, on the other hand, is accompanied by a little noise or mild cough. Gagging is normal at the start of baby-led weaning and you can expect it to ease up as your baby masters chewing and swallowing solid food.

Choosing the best food for baby-led weaning

In baby-led weaning, you should serve your baby soft food cut into small pieces the size your baby can hold in her fist. Of course, you should ensure that you serve foods that will not pose a risk of choking for your little one. You need not worry about how much your baby eats in the first weeks or month of baby-led weaning. Just ensure that you supplement with breastfeeding or bottle-feeding the whole time and ensure that you are serving a well-rounded diet. Offer foods from each of the groups below to ensure that your baby gets all the nutrients she needs:

- Grains e.g whole wheat pasta or wheat toasts with hummus
- Healthy fats e.g. avocados (smeared on bread on eaten directly)
- Protein: boiled beef, chicken, fish (with all the bones removed) and eggs
- Vegetables and fruits: banana, steamed broccoli or carrots, sweet potato fries, etc
- Diary: soft pasteurized cheese and yogurt.

Focus on serving your baby only food with nutritional value. Hence there is no need for sugar, salt or any artificial sweeteners as they only mask the innate natural flavor of food with no real nutritional benefit. Starting with salt and sugar consistently in baby food can also lead to a preference for food unhealthy levels of salt and sugar in later years. It is also recommended that you avoid junk food or prepackaged meals as they are typically nutrient deficient with lots of additives.

Baby-led weaning safety tips

Baby-led weaning is safe for babies as long as they are the appropriate age and you present healthy and baby-safe food. Here are some additional safety tips to keep in mind.

- Don't serve foods that may constitute a choking hazard such as nuts, apples with skin, cherries, and whole grapes

- Don't leave your baby alone with the food. You should still keep an eye on your baby while eating

- Watch out for possible allergic reactions; this is not to say you should hold back certain food for fear of allergies. One of the advantages of trying out a variety of foods is that it reduces the chances of allergies in the future.

- Explain what baby-led weaning to all your baby's caregivers so that they can follow the same safety precautions that you follow.

Baby-led weaning is an interesting approach for introducing solid food to your baby and offers lots of benefits. However, it doesn't mean you are a weaning failure if you prefer to feed your baby pureed food. In fact, some babies may not enjoy baby-led weaning and would do better with conventional methods. The fact is, there is no absolute right way to introduce solid foods to your kid since what may work for one might not work for another baby. It is up to you as a parent to observe your little one and determine the best approach that will guarantee the best results.

RECICPES

SINGLE FIRST FOODS

Sweet Potato Wedges

Time: 40 minutes | Amount: Serves 3

Ingredients:

♦ Sweet potatoes (3 medium)
♦ Olive oil (1/3 c)
♦ Fresh rosemary (2 tbsp)
♦ Pepper
♦ Salt (not compulsory)

How to prepare:

1. Get your oven ready by preheating to a temperature of 200oC or 400oF
2. Wash the sweet potatoes thoroughly, slice into halves then cut them into ba-by-fist sized wedges
3. Toss the wedges into the pan of olive oil. Add pepper and fresh rosemary. You may add little salt if desired
4. Place seasoned wedges on baking sheet (place the skin-side down) down.
5. Place in oven and leave to bake for 30 minutes
6. Turn off the oven and remove. Leave to cool before serving.

Baked Apple Slices

Time: 30 minutes | Amount: Serves 3

Ingredients:

- Apple slices (3)
- Butter (6 tbsp)
- Sugar (1/3 cup)
- Cinnamon (2 tbsp)
- Sea salt (not compulsory)

How to prepare:

1. Prepare oven by preheating to 350oF or 160oC
2. Toss apple slices with butter, cinnamon and sugar in a small baking dish till the apple slices are well coated
3. Place apple slices on baking sheet.
4. Place baking sheet in prehated oven and bake for about 25 minutes or until tender.
5. Leave to cool then serve.

Roasted Broccoli Florets

Time: 30 minutes | Amount: Serves 4

Ingredients:

♦ Broccoli (7 oz/160g)

♦ Olive oil (1 tsp)

♦ Ground black pepper (a pinch)

♦ Sea salt (not compulsory)

How to prepare:

1. Prepare oven by preheating to about 200oC or 400oF.

2. Cut broccoli florets from its stalk

3. Peel each stalk and slice them into baby fist sized slices

4. In a large bowl, mix pieces of florets and talk with some olive oil. Ensure they are well coated.

5. Transfer to the baking sheet then add pepper and salt if desired

6. Put in the preheated oven and roast till the broccoli are tenderized and slightly browned. This should take about 18 minutes or less.

7. Serve

Melon Slices

Time: 5minutes | Amount: Serving 1

Ingredients:

♦ 2 slices of Melon cantaloupe or honeydew

How to prepare:

1. Cut 1/4 of a 7-inch melon (cantaloupe or honeydew) into small baby-fist sizes
2. Place the melon slices on a serving plate then serve

Avocado Toasts

Time: 10 minutes | Amount: Servings 2

Ingredients:

♦ A slice of multigrain bread
♦ Extra virgin olive oil (2 tbsp)
♦ Garlic (1/2 clove)
♦ Avocado (1 large)

How to prepare:

1. Toast bread in toaster or broil it for 1 or 2 minutes on both sides
2. Drizzle each bread toast slice oil while still warm. Rub bread on both sides with the cut side of the garlic
3. With the peel still on, cut avocado slices and remove the pit carefully using a knife
4. Scoop about 1.4 of the avocado on each side of the piece of bread.
5. Using a fork, mash avocado on top of each bread slice.
6. Slice the other side half of avocado while it is still in its peel. Use a spoon to scoop out the slices and spread evenly on the bread slice
7. You can add some salt if desired but this is not recommended for baby food
8. Cut into baby-fist sized pieces and serve.

Baked Avocado Fries

Time: 15 minutes | Amount: Servings 3

Ingredients:

♦ Avocados (2 large or 4 small)
♦ Flour (1/4 c)
♦ Milk (1/2 c)
♦ Garlic powder (1/4 tsp)
♦ Breadcrumbs (1 cup)- if desired

How to prepare:

1. Get oven ready by preheating to 400o|F or 200oC

2. Prepare baking sheet by greasing with oil then leave aside

3. Mix garlic and flour in a small shallow dish

4. Cut and peel avocado then coat each slice in flour mixture

5. Dip coated slice in flour then dip in milk

6. Sprinkle breadcrumbs on each slice then press down lightly until the bread-crumbs stick on the Avocado slices

7. Place slices on baking tray then place in oven for about 15 minutes or until tenderized.

8. Remove from oven and serve. You can store leftover in the freezer for up to 3 days.

Dark Meat Chicken

Time: 1hour |Amount: Servings 6

Ingredients:

♦ Soy sauce(3 tbsp)

♦ Honey (5 tbsp)

♦ Olive oil (3 tbsp)

♦ Garlic (3 cloves)

♦ Ground pepper (1/2 tsp)

♦ Ground ginger (1/2 tsp)

♦ Chicken thighs (with the bone in) or a big piece that baby can suck on

How to prepare:

1. Preheat the oven 200oC/400oF

7. Mix Ingredients (except chicken) in a ziploc bag then add chicken to the bag.

2. Seal and mix until chicken is well coated.

3. You can leave chicken to marinate for some minutes till you are ready to begin cooking.

4. Add the chicken along with the marinade in a baking sheet. (position with the skin-side up)

5. Bake in oven for 25 minutes. Turn over chicken then cook for an additional 10 minutes.

6. Turn chicken again then cook for 10 minutes more

7. Serve chicken piece with bone still in (for easy holding) or a large piece that baby can suck on.

Baked Salmon Bites

Time: 20 minutes | Amount:8 bites

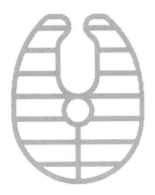

Ingredients:

♦ salmon fillet (200g/7oz)
♦ Ground almond (1/3 cup)
♦ Mayonnaise (2 tbsp)

How to prepare:

1. Remove bones from salmon fillets then cut into small baby-fist sized chunks

2. Place salmon chunks in a large bowl then add mayonnaise. Roll the salmon pieces around in bowl until sufficiently coated.

3. Place the coated salmon pieces in a bowl containing the ground almond. Roll the pices in this bowl until well coated with the ground almond as well

4. Place salmon bits on a prepared tray lined with baking sheets

5. Bake in oven at about 180oC or 380oF for 10 minutes. Turn over using a tong and continue to bake for 5 more minutes.

6. When cooked through, remove from the oven and set aside to cool then serve.

Soft Baked Carrot Recipe

Time: 50 minutes | Amount: 12 servings

Ingredients:

♦ Baby carrots thoroughly washed
♦ Olive oil

How to prepare:

1. Place carrots on a baking tray. You can grease carrot with oil or simply use a cassarole dish instead if you desire to avoid oil entirely.

2. Get oven ready by preheating to about 177oC/350oF

3. Place tray or dish in prepared oven

4. Bake in oven for 40 minutes until the color of the carrot turns to a dark orange and it is tenderized.

5. Remove baked carrots from oven. Serve when cooled.

Baby French Toast Sticks

Time: 15 minutes | Amount: 6 sticks

Ingredients:

- 2 eggs
- Baby's usual milk (1/2 cup)
- Cinnamon
- Vanilla extract (1 tsp)
- Ginger
- 3 or 4 slices of bread (whole wheat) cut into thick finger shapes
- Butter or oil

How to prepare:

1. In a bowl, mix the eggs, vanilla, ginger and cinnamon
2. Cut bread into finger shapes (about 3 slices per bread)
3. Melt butter or oil in a pan.
4. Place the pieces of bread into egg mixture to coat. Transfer coated pieces to the pan.
5. Cook in melted butter for 3 minutes on each side. Repeat this for each bread stick
6. Remove french toast. Set side on a place and serve when cooled.

WHAT TO FEED ON THE GO

Banana Blender Pancakes

Time: 15 minutes | Amount: 12 pancakes

Ingredients:

♦ Banana (1-2)
♦ Greek style yogurt (1.2 cup)
♦ Egg (1)
♦ Honey or maple syrup (1 tbsp)
♦ Vanilla essence (1 tsp)
♦ Butter or oil (for greasing pan)

How to prepare:

1. Put all Ingredients: into blender and turn on. Whizz until you have a smooth batter.
2. Pour batter into greased pan then cook for a while on medium heat.
3. Flip when you notice bubbles begin to appear on the surface of pancakes
4. Continue to cook till both sides of the pancake has a golden-brown color
5. Set aside and serve when cooled.

Baby Apple and Oats Pancakes

Time:8 mins | Amount: 12 yields

Ingredients:

- Rolled oats (1.5 cups)
- Vanilla extract(1 tsp)
- Apple puree (1/2 cup)
- Baking soda (1/2 tsp)
- Milk (1/2 cup)
- Baking powder (1 tsp)
- Maple syrup (1 tbsp)

How to prepare:

1. Blitz oats until fine using a food processor or blender
2. Add remaining ingredient and blend again until you have a smooth and thick mixture
3. Drop batter in spoonfuls onto a medium greased pan
4. Flip pancakes when you notice bubbles begin to form on the surface.
5. Cook until the color turns light brown
6. Remove from heat and set aside for a few minutes before you serve.

Simple Banana Oats Cookies

Time: 35 minutes | Amount: 20 cookies

Ingredients:

♦ Chia seeds (1 tbsp)

♦ Banana (3)

♦ Oats (1.5 cups)

♦ Plain flour (1/2c)

How to prepare:

1. Pour chia seeds into water. Leave seeds in the water for about 10 minutes. (the seeds should form a gel by this time

2. Mash banana in a medium bowl.

3. To the bowl of banana stir vanilla and the soaked chia seeds

4. Add in the flour and oats then mix thoroughly to form a cookie dough. The dough should have a moist and sticky texture

5. Scoop mixture with a table spoon and place onto a tray lined with baking sheets. It may be difficult to form perfect shapes since the mix will be sticky.

6. Bake the cookies in an oven25 minutes at 180oC or 360oF.

7. Remove from oven and leave till it is cool enough to serve. The cookies should begin to soften by now.

8. It can be served immediately. You an store for serving on the go for up to 2 to 3 days inside a cookie jar (may be frozen up for as much as 3 months and thawed when needed).

Sweet Corn and Spinach Fritters

Time: 15 minutes | Amount:12 fritters

Ingredients:

- Salt-free sweetcorn (1 can, 200g/7oz)
- Bay spinach leaf (a small handful)
- Spring onion (1, chopped)
- Garlic clove (1)
- Baking powder (1/2 tsp)
- Plain four (50g/2oz)
- 1 egg
- Milk (50ml)
- Rapeseed (1 tsp)-for frying

How to prepare:

1. Pulse all your Ingredients: or food processor (except the oil). blend until it is fairly smooth.

2. Heat some oil in a frying pan until hot.

3. Dollop spoonfuls of batter into the oil. Be sure to leave enough space around them

4. Fry in oil for about a minute on each side until the fritters begin to form a light golden color. Flatten fritters with a spatula until evenly cooked. Repeat this for all the batter.

5. Place cooked fritters in a bowl or plate. Serve when warm or cool enough for baby to handle.

6. Fritters can be stored frozen and reheated in an oven when needed.

Simple Chicken Cashew Satay on Lolly Sticks

Time: 15 minutes | Amount: 3 sticks

Ingredients:

♦ Chicken breast (1 large) cut into 9 chunks
♦ Rapeseed oil (1 tsp)
♦ Garlic clove (1, crushed)
♦ Cashew nut butter (1.5 tbsp)
♦ Low-salt soy sauce (1 tsp)
♦ Coconut milk (50ml) mixed with 2 tbsp of water
♦ Honey (1 tsp)

How to prepare:

1. Heat oven to 360oF/180oC
2. Feed chicken chunks into 3 lolly sticks (3 per stick)
3. Arrange the chicken on prepare baking tray then place in the oven.
4. Bake in oven for 10 minutes until tender and cooked through
5. Remove chicken from oven and leave aside to cool. Serve when warm.

RECIPES WITH VEGETABLES

Lentil & Sweet Potato Croquettes

Time: 1 hour 40 mins | Amount: 14 Croquettes

Ingredients:

- ♦ Olive oil (1 tbsp)
- ♦ Red onion (1)
- ♦ Carrot (1, large)
- ♦ Sweet potato (1, medium)
- ♦ Red lentils (100g/3.5oz)
- ♦ Breadcrumbs (90g/3oz)
- ♦ 1 egg
- ♦ Low organic stock cube (1)
- ♦ Water (500ml)

How to prepare:

1. Chop the onion, sweet potato and carrot into small chunks
2. Pour oil in a pan then heat up. Add chopped onions, carrots & garlic then saute.
3. Add in the sweet potato and lentil then add water till mixture if fully covered.
4. Bring the water to boil and add stock cube.
5. Cover pan and leave to simmer on low heat for 30 minutes. Stir regularly as you cook.
6. Add in some more water as the mixture become thicker
7. Check to see if carrots and sweet potatoes are softened then remove mixture from the heat.
8. Form a puree by mashing the mixture set mixture aside for about 30 minutes till it cools.
9. Preheat oven to 190oC or 390oF.
10. Pour pureed mixture into a large bowl, add in cheese and egg and stir the mixture. Add about half of breadcrumbs to make the mixture thicker.
11. Form a croquette with a heaped tablespoon of mixture. Do this for the rest of the mixture. You should have about 14 croquettes in all when you are done.
12. Roll each of the croquette in the remaining breadcrumbs then place on a pre-pared baking tray.
13. Place croquettes in an oven then bake for 30 minutes until it turns a golden brown color.
14. Remove croquette from oven and leave to cool
15. Can be served immediately or stored in the freezer in an airtight container for up to 5 days. Keep in a zip lock bag once frozen.

Salmon Sweet Potato Fritters

Time: 35 minutes | Amount: 15 to 20 fritters

Ingredients:

- Salmon (3/4 lb/0.3kg) roughly chopped with the bones and skin removed
- Cooked sweet potato(1, medium)
- 1 egg
- Onion (1/2, diced)
- Olive oil (1 tbsp, +more for cooking)
- minced garlic (3 cloves)
- Minced ginger (2 tbsp)
- Oats (1 1/4 cups)
- Minced Baby spinach (2 cups)

How to prepare:

1. Preheat your oven to about 350oF/160oC

2. Add 1 tablespoon of oil into a skillet over medium high heat. To the skillet, add ginger, garlic an onion. Leave to saute, stiring continously for about 2 minutes until softened.

3. Transfer to a food processor and return pan to the heat.

4. To the pan, add spinach and cook for 2 minutes until spinach wilts then set aside.

5. Add salmon, egg, cooked potato (with the skin discarded) and oats to the food processor. Also add garlic, ginger and onion. Pulse this mixture until when mixed then add spinach and pulse again.

6. Coat your fingers with some oil and also grease the pan. Roll mixture with your hands to form fritters then fry in the pan till they turn a golden brown color.

7. Transfer fritters to baking sheet. Repeat this for all the mixture. Place sheet in an oven then cook for 10 minutes.

8. Remove from oven and leave to cook. To be served slightly warm.

Vegetable Quinoa Biscuits for Baby

Time: 30 minutes | Amount: 4 portions

Ingredients:

♦ Shredded organic zucchini (1 cup)
♦ Cooked quinoa (2 cups)
♦ Organic carrots (shredded, 2 cups)
♦ Cheddar cheese (1 cup)
♦ Parsley (1/4 cup)
♦ 3 eggs

How to prepare:

1. Prepare oven by preheating to about 350oF/160oC
2. Beat eggs and add all the ingredient in a large bowl and mix gently until they are well combined.
3. Scoop a quarter of the mixture with a measuring cup into a baking sheet. Repeat until all the mixture is used up.
4. Place the baking sheet in preheated oven and bake for 20 minutes.
5. Once done, remove form oven and serve when cool.

Vegan Sesame and Soy Cauliflower Wings

Time: 50 minutes | Amount: 2 adults and 2 babies

Ingredients:

- Cauliflower (1/2 large head)
- Flour (1 cup)
- Garam masala (1/2 tsp)
- Black pepper (to season)
- Paprika (2tsp)
- Water (1 cup)

Rapeseed oil sauce

- Maple syrup (2 tbsp)
- Low salt soy sauce (1.5 tbsp)
- Sesame oil (1 tbsp)
- Rapeseed oil (1 tbsp)
- Juice from 1 lime

How to prepare:

1. Prepare oven by preheating to 180oC/360oF

2. Cut cauliflower into floret then wash and dry of

3. Add flour, garam masala, pepper and paprika into a bowl then stir.

4. Make a pit in the center of the mixture. Add in oil then water and mix well until a smooth batter is formed (you can add a little more water if the batter seems to be too thick.

5. Add cauliflower to this batter then stir until completely covered. Take each piece of cauliflower out then shake off any excess batter on it.

6. Line a baking tray with parchment sheets.

7. Place cauliflower on the parchment paper then cook in the oven for 25 minutes. The batter should be crispy when it is done

8. To prepare sauce put all the Ingredients: in a pot and bring to boil. Leave for about five minute to bubble and for the sauce to thicken like a thick caramel.

9. Remove pot from the heat and leave to cool for about 5 minutes.

10. Pour sauce over cauliflower and toss then return into the oven for 10 additional minutes.

11. Turn off the oven and remove cauliflower wings then serve.

Cheese Vegetable Muffins

Time: 35minutes | Amount: 24 mini-muffins (12 regular size)

Ingredients:

♦ Milk (250ml)

♦ 2 eggs

♦ Rapeseed oil (60ml)

♦ Baking powder (2 tsp)

♦ Plain flour (300g)

♦ Grated carrots (3 medium)

♦ Grated courgette (1 medium)

♦ Finely chopped spinach leaves (2 handfuls)

♦ Cheddar cheese (70g/3oz)

How to prepare:

1. Prepare oven by preheating to 200°C/400°F

2. Whisk eggs, rapeseed oil & milk in a bowl.

3. To the mixture in the bowl, add flour slowly and mix. Also add black pepper and baking powder and mix until a smooth batter is formed

4. Add cheese and veggies while you continue to mix until Ingredients: are well combined

5. Place in preheated oven and leave to bake for 24 minutes till the muffins turn a golden brown color.

6. Remove muffins form oven and leave to cool in the tin for about 5 minutes before removing,

7. Serve muffins when they are cool enough for baby to handle. They can be stored for about a week frozen in an airtight container.

Kid Friendly Chicken Cobb Salad on a Stick

Time: 40 minutes | Amount:4 servings

Ingredients:

- Roasted chicken breasts (2)
- Paprika (2 tsp)
- Ground coriander (1/2 tsp)
- Black pepper
- Rapeseed oil
- Lettuce (1 head, small)
- Cherry tomatoes (4, halved)
- Baby avocados (2)
- Sauce
- Yogurt (200ml)
- Goat cheese (60g/2oz)

How to prepare:

1. Cut the chicken breasts into manageable chunks for a baby to handle and place in the pan.

2. Add the spices, rapeseed oil and pepper.

3. Turn the heat on and stir the mixture till the chicken is well coated. The outside of the chicken should be crispy. Turn down heat and leave aside to cool.

4. Make skewers using a piece of chicken, lettuce leave, halved tomato, a piece of avocado and egg. Repeat this for all Ingredients:

5. Prepare the sauce by pouring yogurt in a small bowl. Mash in the soft goat cheese then stir until smooth and creamy

6. Drizzle over the skewers and serve

Baby Friendly Cranberry, Pesto and Goat Cheese Bites

Time:30 minutes | Amount:36 bites

Ingredients:

- Plain flour (200g/7oz)
- Butter (75g/3oz)
- Water (2 tbsp)
- Pesto (100g/3.5oz)
- Goat cheese (150g/5oz)
- Finely chopped rosemary (2 sprigs)
- Desiccated coconut (1 tbsp)

How to prepare:

1. Prepare oven by preheating to 400oF or 180°C

2. Mix butter & flour in a bowl with your hands until it resembles breadcrumbs.

3. Add some water and mix some more to form a dough

4. Add some extra flour to your work surface then roll dough. Cut dough into small circles using a cookie cutter

5. Place cookies onto a baking tray lined with baking sheets then bake for about 15 minutes until color turns golden

6. On each cookie, spoon about half a teaspoon of pesto then top with goat cheese. Return pastry to oven and bake for 5 more minutes until goat cheese melts

7. Top with some cranberry sauce and add a sprinkle of coconut and cranberry before serving.

Pitta Pockets with Quinoa Salad

Time: 25 minutes | Amount: serves 2 adults and 2 kids

Ingredients:

- Quinoa (130g/4.5oz)-cooked (follow the directions on the pack)
- Diced avocado (1/2)
- Finely-chopped onions(3)
- Diced cucumber (1/4)
- Mint leaves (8, finely chopped)
- Black pepper

For Dressing

- roasted garlic (2 cloves)
- Extra-virgin olive oil (2 tbsp)
- Maple syrup (1 tsp)
- Grated ginger (1/4 tsp)
- Lemon zest & juice form one lemon

For Yogurt Sauce

- Natural yogurt
- Mint leaves (4)
- Black pepper

How to prepare:

1. Place cooked quinoa in a bowl

2. To the bowl, add mint leaves and chopped veggies

3. Add in all the Ingredients: for the dressing in a food processor/blender. Turn the processor on and blitz until smooth.

4. Pour processed dressing over quinoa and vegetables then mix till combined.

5. To prepare yogurt sauce, stir all the Ingredients: together

6. Heat pittas in a toaster until soft, cut in half and fill each side with the prepared quinoa salad. Add a little sauce to top and serve.

Baby Friendly Minestrone Soup

Time: 1 hour | Amount: Serves 2 adults and 2 kids

Ingredients:

- Olive oil (1.4 cup)
- Finely diced onion (1 large)
- Cloves of garlic (4, crushed)
- Carrots (2 large)
- Courgette (1)
- Celery (1 stick)
- Fresh thyme leaves (6 sprigs)
- English mustard (1 tsp)
- Tomatoes (400g/14oz tin)
- Tomato puree (4 tsp)
- 6 tomatoes
- Water (1.5liters)
- Butter beans (2 tins, 400g/14oz each)
- Macaroni pasta shells (2.5 cups)
- Black pepper
- Fresh thyme leaves
- Grated goat cheese

How to prepare:

1. Heat oil and fry onions in a large pot until onions become translucent. Add in garlic then cook for 1 additional minute.

2. Add vegetables (cut into spears) then stir fry until they are slightly softened. Add in thyme leaves, tomato purer, tomato, mustard and some water then stir until well combined.

3. Cool until it begins to bubble then cover and simmer for 30 minutes.

4. Add pasta, butterbeans and a little pepper to season. Cover pot and cook for 10 minutes till the pasta is cooked.

5. Add in tomatoes and cook for 10 more minutes to soften.

6. Serve soup with goat cheese and basil leaves sprinkled on.

Cauliflower Cheese Cakes

Time: 30 minutes | Amount: Serves 4

Ingredients:

♦ Oil
♦ Cauliflower (1/2 head)-cut into florets
♦ Brown bread (1 slice) cut into chunks
♦ 1 egg
♦ Grated cheddar cheese (50g/2oz)
♦ Chives (a few, snipped)

How to prepare:

1. Get oven ready by preheating to 180C/380F.
2. Prepare the baking tray by lining with a baking sheet or foil. Brush sheets with oil.
3. Place cauliflower in a steamer then place over boil water for 8 minutes until tender. Remove from steamer and leave to cool.
4. Put bread in a food processor then blitz to form crumbs. To this, add the egg, cauliflower, chives, grated cheese & black pepper then pulse until the mixture become chunky
5. Form paste into patties (about 8) and arrange on baking tray
6. Bake in the oven for 20 minutes until the color turns golden and the patties are crisp around the edges.
7. Remove from oven and serve cooled.

DINNER RECIPES

Chicken and Broccoli Pasta Bake

Time: 50 minutes | Amount:4 servings (2 adults and 2 kids)

Ingredients:

- Pasta (300g/10oz)
- 2 Aubergine
- Rapeseed oil (a splash)
- 1 Finely chopped onion
- Crushed garlic (2 cloves)
- Chicken breasts (3, diced)
- Whole milk (2 cups)
- Fresh cream (1/4c)
- Greek yogurt (1/4c)
- Basil leaves (a handful)
- Goat cheese (2 tbsp)

How to prepare:

1. Preheat your oven to about 180oC/380oF

2. Cook pasta following the instructions on the pack. Drain water from pasta and leave aside.

3. Slice aubergine, place the sliced pieces on baking tray lined with parchment sheet. Add a little quantity of rapeseed oil then place in oven and bake for 15 minutes until softened.

4. In a large pot, heat rapeseed oil then add garlic and onion. Gently fry for some minutes.

5. Add chicken breasts to pot and cook till cooked through. Add in broccoli then cook for 5 minutes

6. Pour in milk, cream, yogurt and the goat cheese then stir until a creamy sauce is formed. To the sauce, add in pasta then stir.

7. Add mixture to baking tray then top with roasted aubergine and the tomatoes, add some cheese then

8. Bake in oven for 25 minutes till it turns to a golden color.

9. Remove from oven and leave to cool before serving warm.

Veggie Loaded Irish Stew

Time:1 10 minutes | Amount: 4 servings

Ingredients:

- Rapeseed oil
- 325g/12oz beef strips
- 2 carrots
- 1 onion
- cumin seeds (1 tsp)
- Ginger (thumbsize)
- 2 cloves garlic
- Flour (1 tbsp)
- 2 cloves garlic
- Tomato puree (2 tbsp)
- Water (1L)
- Red pepper (2)
- Chopped tomatoes (1 can)
- Baby potatoes (1 kg/35oz)
- Kale (a handful)
- Sprig rosemary

How to prepare:

1. Heat rapeseed oil in a pan and turn heat up to medium.

2. Add beef to pan and cook for 3 minutes until browned. Set beef aside in bowl.

3. Add onions and carrots to the same pan and cook for some minutes until onions start to turn translucent. Add cumin seed, garlic and ginger then cook for 1 minute.

4. Add in flour and tomato puree then add water slowly while stirring continuously until well combined

5. Chop pepper & add to mixture. Also chop the kale and baby potatoes and add as well along the finely chopped rosemary sprig

6. Return meat to the pot, and simmer on low heat with the pot covered for about 1 hour.

7. Turn heat down & serve. Best enjoyed warm.

Lemon Broccoli Pasta Skillet

Time: 20 minutes | Amount: 6 servings

Ingredients:

♦ Water (3 quarts)

♦ Fresh broccoli (2 lbs/0.9kg)

♦ Spinach (3 cups)

♦ Butter (4 tbsp)

♦ Juice and zest from 1 lemon

♦ Crushed red pepper

♦ 2 cloves Crushed & minced garlic

♦ Olive oil (to garnish)

♦ Fresh lemon (to garnish)

How to prepare:

1. Boil water in a large skillet or pot.
2. Prep broccoli by trimming stems and cutting the florets into smaller pieces
3. Add rotini to water and continue to boil for 4 minutes. Add broccoli to the boiling water. Leave covered for 3 additional minutes before turning heat off.
4. Drain pasta with a colander then return to pan and stir in spinach.
5. Melt butter in a skillet over medium heat.
6. To this, add red pepper and minced garlic then saute for about a minute until fragrant.
7. Turn off the heat then add 2 to 3 tbsp of lemon juice. Add in your to your pasta and stir
8. Stir in Parmesan cheese and add a drizzle of oil. Season to taste
9. Serve garnished with cheese and lemon wedges.

Pesto Chicken and Broccoli Pasta

Time: 25 minutes | Amount: Serves 4

Ingredients:

- ♦ Minced onion (1/2)
- ♦ Olive oil
- ♦ Minced garlic (4)
- ♦ Chicken breasts (2, cut into strips)
- ♦ Light cream (1 cup)
- ♦ Parmesan cheese (1/4, grated)
- ♦ Pesto (1/4 c)
- ♦ Aldante (4c)
- ♦ Broccoli florets (1c)

How to prepare:

1. Follow the instructions on the packaging to cook pasta

2. Add broccoli into the pasta one minute before you turn off the heat. Drain then set aside

3. While you are cooking pasta, pour 1 table spoon of olive oil into a large pan. Cook onions in oil for 3 minutes until it turns a golden color.

4. To this, add in garlic then cook for an additional minute before adding the strips of chicken breast.

5. Season with salt and pepper as desired and cook for about 5 minutes till browned.

6. Add in Parmesan cheese, cream and pesto then cook for 3 more minutes.

7. Add cooked broccoli and pasta then stir until well mixed. Continue to simmer for 3 minutes before turning off heat.

8. To be served garnished with Parmesan

Slow Cooker Chickpea Sweet Potato Korma

Time: 4 hours 10 mins | Amount:4 servings (2 adults and 2 kid)

Ingredients:

- Onions (2 medium)
- Ginger (1, thumb size)
- Garlic (3 cloves)
- Rapeseed oil (3 tbsp)
- Chopped tomatoes (1 tin)
- Tomato puree (4 tbsp)
- Coconut milk (1 tin)
- Garam masala (1 tsp)
- Turmeric (1 tsp)
- Coriander (1 tbsp)
- Maple syrup (2 tsp)
- Chickpeas (2 tsp)
- Cumin seeds (1 tsp)
- Frozen peas (300g/12oz)
- Sweet potato(16oz)

How to prepare:

1. Cook roughly chopped onions, ginger & garlic in a slow cooker with rapeseed oil until the onions turn translucent

2. Add in the tin of tomatoes and the tomato puree. Blend using a stick blender till it is creamy and smooth.

3. Add in coconut milk, maple syrup, chickpeas and spices until well mixed

4. Peel sweet potatoes and chop into large chunks

5. Place pot into slow cooker and turn on the heat to medium then cook for 4 hours. Alternatively you can cook in an oven at 150oC/300oF in an oven dish covered with tin foil

6. The potatoes should be soft by the time you are done.

7. Add frozen peas about 10 minutes to the end of cooking

8. Remove from cooker or oven and leave to cool

Fussy Eater Vegetable Pizza

Time:25 minutes | Amount:4 servings

Ingredients:

For pizza dough

- warm water (250ml)
- Olive oil (3 tbsp)
- Dried yeast (7g/0.4oz)
- White flour (320g)

For sauce

- Rapeseed oil
- Tomato puree (unsalted, 150g/5oz)
- Crushed garlic c(1 clove)
- Roughly chopped courgette (1)
- Roughly chopped red pepper (1)
- Tomatoes (1/2 tin)

For toppings

- Onion (1 large, sliced)
- Baby leaf spinach (2 handfuls, finely chopped)
- Red bell peppers (2)
- Mozzarella (2 packs)
- Grated Mozzarella

How to prepare:

1. To prepare dough, add some warm water and oil into a jug then add in maple syrup and yeast. Whisk until well mixed then lay aside for 10 minutes until yeast activates.

2. Sieve flour and pour into a bowl. Make a pit in the middle of the dry flour with your hands.

3. Slowly pour in water and yeast mixture then stir with your hands or dough mixer. Continue to mix to form a dough.

4. Turn the dough out onto a floured countertop. Dip your hands in flour & knead the dough for about 13 minutes until it is springy & soft.

5. After kneading, place dough in a floured bowl and leave covered for about 60 minutes in a warm place. The dough should rise and double in size.

6. Meanwhile, prepare your sauce and fillings as the dough is proving

7. Turn dough back onto your counter top and knead again for a while to get rid of any air from it.

8. Cut dough into 4 parts (3 parts for the adult pizzas and 1 for 24 baby-sized pizzas)

9. To prepare sauce, pour all the Ingredients: for the sauce into a frying pan and cook for 8 to 10 minutes until they are softened. Use a stick blender to mix Ingredients: till smooth then set aside to cool.

10. Preheat oven.

11. Roll each piece of dough as flat as possible using a rolling pin.

12. Place each piece on a pizza stone or baking tray and add some tablespoon of sauce. Add topping and mozzarella

13. Bake dough for about 12 minutes until pizza is not doughy anymore.

Turkey Stuffing Muffins

Time:35 minutes | Amount: 24 muffins

Ingredients:

- Wholegrain breadcrumbs (4 cups)
- Finely diced onion (1, medium)
- Finely chopped sage leaves (4)
- Rosemary leaves (1 large sprig, finely chopped)
- Melted butter (1/3 cup)
- Cooked broccoli (2 cups, chop finely)
- Cooked turkey breast (diced, 2.5 cups)
- 5 eggs
- Cranberry sauce

How to prepare:

1. Get oven ready by preheating to 400oF/180oC
2. Put in all the Ingredients: (except eggs) in a large bowl & mix thoroughly.
3. In a separate bowl, mix eggs till they are fluffy and light then pour mixture over bread and veggie mixture.
4. Stir the mixture well then divide into oiled muffin tins
5. Bake muffins in oven for 25 to 30 minutes until the top turns crispy.
6. Serve muffins with cranberry sauce or on its own.

Finger Fish Fruit Cakes

Time: 30 minutes | Amount:4 servings

Ingredients:

- ◆ Rapeseed oil
- ◆ Red onion (1 medium, roughly choped)
- ◆ Garlic (2 cloves)
- ◆ juice and zest from 1 lime
- ◆ Turmeric, coriander and cumin (1 tsp)
- ◆ Hake fillets (2 large)- make sure you remove the bones
- ◆ 1 egg
- ◆ Fresh coriander (a handful)
- ◆ Flour (2 tbsp_
- ◆ Green beans
- ◆ Breadcrumbs
- ◆ Greek yogurt (2 tbsp)
- ◆ Juice from 1/4 lime
- ◆ Parsley

How to prepare:

1. Heat oil in frying pan then add onion and fry till color turns golden

2. Crush garlic and add to oil then fry for two additional minutes until well cooked

3. Pour mixture in a food processor. Add some limes, fish, spices, coriander and egg and blend until mixture is broken up and smooth.

4. Pour mixture into a large bowl along with the flour.

5. Slice green beans finely and add to this mixture then stir

6. Form the mixture into cakes. Drop and roll cakes in breadcrumbs. Repeat for all of the mixture.

7. Fry cakes in rapeseed oil until both sides turn a golden color and are cooked though.

8. Serve with a mixture of greek yogurt and lime juice then sprinkle with parsley to garnish.

Mini Baby-Friendly Quiches

Time: 40 minutes | Amount:4 servings

Ingredients:

♦ Plain flour (2 cups)

♦ Butter (120g/4oz)

♦ Water (3 to 4 tsp)

♦ Rapeseed oil

♦ Onion (1 medium)

♦ Garlic (3 cloves, crushed)

♦ Finely chopped spinach leaves (1 handful)

♦ Cherry tomatoes (24, quartered)

♦ Fresh basil leaves (a handful)

♦ 4 eggs

♦ Cheddar cheese (100g/3.5oz)

How to prepare:

1. Get oven ready by preheating to 180oC/400oF

2. Sieve flour into a bowl. Then butter and mix with the flour using your hands until the mixture look like breadcrumbs

3. Add water to this mixture (one tsp at a time) then mix until a sticky dough is formed

4. Pour dough on a floured surface then roll until thined. Shape out mini circular cookies with a cookie cutter then leave in the refrigerator until you are ready to start filling.

5. In a frying pan, heat oil then pour in onions. Fry gently until onions become translucent.

6. To the frying onion, add spinach & garlic. Cook for 3 minutes until spinach wilts.

7. Add chopped basil leaves and cherry tomatoes,

8. Remove pastry from fridge then add in a tsp of the mixture to each

9. In a jug or bowl, whisk egg until fluffy and light. Fill each quiche up with egg and add some cheddar cheese.

10. Put quiches in oven and bake for about 25 minutes till egg sets

11. Turn off oven and set quiches aside till it is cool enough to serve.

Veggie Loaded Spaghetti Bolognese

Time: 40 minutes | Amount:4 servings (2 adult and 2 children)

Ingredients:

- Onions (2 medium)
- Olive oil (3 tbsp)
- Garlic (4 cloves)
- Roughly chopped courgette
- Diced red pepper (2)
- Frozen peas (2 cups)
- Spinach leaves (3 handfuls)
- Chopped tomatoes (2 tins)
- Tomato puree (4 tbsp)
- Water (200ml)
- Black pepper (added to season)
- Cherry tomatoes (15)
- Cooked spaghetti
- Fresh basil leaves (a handful)
- Goat cheese (grated)

How to prepare:

1. Chop onions roughly then heat in oil over medium high heat until onions turn translucent.

2. Add in garlic and courgette, pepper and the frozen peas. Stir & cook for 5 minutes until Ingredients: soften.

3. Turn heat down & add spinach leaves, tomato puree, tins of tomato, pepper (a little) & water.

4. Blend mixture with a stick blender until mixture is creamy and smooth. Turn heat on and add the remaining pepper. Leave to simmer for 15 to 20 minutes until sauce thickens to your preference.

5. Quarter cherry tomatoes and sprinkle into sauce. Cook for an additional 5 minutes.

6. Serve with cooked spaghetti and a sprinkle of basil and grated goat cheese.

Potato Salad

Time: 45 minutes | Amount:8 servings (4 adult and 4 children)

Ingredients:

♦ Baby potatoes (1kg/2lbs)

♦ Garlic (4 cloves)

♦ Black pepper

♦ Oil (2 tbsp)

♦ Zest from one lemon

♦ Paprika (1 tsp)

♦ Apple cider vinegar (1 tbsp)

♦ Parsley (30g/1oz)

♦ Sour cream (100ml)

♦ Natural yogurt (100ml)

How to prepare:

1. Add garlic loves and baby potatoes into a pot then add water until completely covered

2. Bring water to boil then turn heat down. Simmer with the pot covered for 10 to 15 minute till potatoes tenderize.

3. Drain and remove garlic cloves then set aside

4. To the pot, add olive oil, lemon zest, black pepper, vinegar and paprika. Toss potatoes until well coated then leave to cool fully.

5. Place coated potatoes in a bowl. Add parsley and finely chopped onions to bowl. Also add in yogurt and sour cream then stir to mix

6. Leave to cool and serve.

Meatless Meatballs

Time: 45 minutes | Amount: 4 servings (2 adults and 2 kids)

Ingredients:

- Olive oil (1/4 cup)
- Roughly chopped onino (1 medium)
- Crushed garlic (2 cloves)
- Chickpeas (2 tins)
- Basil leaves (1 handful)
- Thyme leaves (2 sprigs)
- Breadcrumbs (1.5 cups)
- 2 eggs
- English mustard (1 tsp)
- Garlic bread
- Ciabatta loaf (1 large)
- Butter (2 tbsp)
- Thyme (2 sprigs)

For Sauce

- Olive oil
- Finely diced onion
- Tomatoes (1 tin)
- Garlic cloves (2, sliced)
- Tomato puree (4 tbsp)
- Apple cider vinegar (1.5 tbsp)

How to prepare:

1. Prepare your oven by heating to 400F/180C

2. Pour oil into a pan then add garlic and onion, frying until translucent.

3. Transfer frying onion and garlic into a blender/food processor. Pour in herbs, breadcrumbs and chickpeas and process for a while until the chickpeas become broken up and forms a dough like mixture.

4. Add eggs to mixture & pulse in the processor until well mixed.

5. Get a baking tray ready by lining it with parchment paper. Scoop the mixture onto the lined backing tray.

6. Place tray in oven and bake for 25 minutes till it forms firm meatballs.

7. To prepare garlic bread, mix butter with thyme and garlic and spread over the bread. Place bread on baking tray and cover with a tin foil. Bake bread for 10 to 15 minutes.

8. To prepare sauce, heat up oil gently and fry onions in oil till softened. Add garlic then cook for a minute until fragrant.

9. To this, add tin of tomato, vinegar & tomato puree. Stir mixture and simmer for about 18 to 20 minute to thicken sauce.

10. When meat balls are cooked, add in sauce then toss to coat.

11. Serve when cool.

Salmon Fish Fingers with Chunky Chips

Time: 30 minutes | Amount: 12 fish fingers

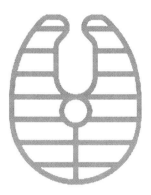

Ingredients:

♦ Potato (2 cut into wedges)

♦ Oil (2 tbsp)

♦ Egg (1 large, beaten)

♦ Breadcrumbs (100g/4oz) made from fresh bread

♦ Smoked paprika

♦ 4 Salmon (remove all the bones)

♦ Salmon fillets

♦ Oil (for drizzling)

♦ Any vegetable

How to prepare:

1. Preheat oven to 180C/380F

2. Place potato wedges on baking sheet then drizzle with oil and toss into the oven (you don't need to season if you are cooking for your baby). Place in oven and bake for 20 to 25 minutes. Turn wedges half-way through cooking.

3. Pout beaten egg into a bowl. Also pour breadcrumbs onto a plate. To this, add smoked paprika & some seasoning if desired.

4. Brush baking sheet with the remaining oil. Dip fish strips first in the egg then in the breadcrumbs until well coated. Transfer this to the baking sheet.

5. Bake fish strips for about 25 minutes until it turns golden then turn off the oven.

6. Carefully lift fish fingers from the tray using a spatula. Serve on a plate with chunky potato chips and your favorite vegetable.

7. The fish fingers can be stored for later use in a freezer and cooked from frozen when needed.

Chicken Meatballs

Time:25 minutes | Amount:16 to 20 meatballs

Ingredients:

♦ Celery (1/2 stick) cut into chunks

♦ Carrot (1, small)

♦ Chicken thighs (boneless and skinless, cut into smaller chunks)-500g/17oz

♦ Chives (a few, snipped)

♦ Oil

How to prepare:

1. Prepare oven by heating to 400F/200C

2. In a blender/food processor, add celery, chicken, carrot and chives and blitz a couple of times.

3. Shape mixture into meatballs. (meatballs can be kept frozen and defrosted when needed) or cook immediately.

4. To cook, place meatballs on a baking tray prepared for the purpose then place in oven. Bake for about 10 to 15 minutes until well cooked and slightly browned.

5. Remove from oven. Can be served with steamed broccoli and rice.

Fish Pie Bites

Time: 1 hour 40 minutes | Amount: 8 bites

Ingredients:

♦ Potato (1, medium)

♦ Salmon fillet (1 small, 120g/5oz)

♦ Chives (1 tsp, snipped into strands)

♦ Grated mild cheddar

♦ Beaten egg (1/2)

♦ Oil

How to prepare:

1. Get oven ready by heating to 200C/400F

2. Wrap potato in foil then place on baking tray. Roast in the oven for about 1hour 15minutes. Wrap fish in the same foil and put on the tray then continue to bake for another 12 minutes until cooked through

3. Halve potato and scoop out filling. Flake fish, remove the skin and any bones in it.

4. Grease baking stray with oil. Mash baked potato and mix with flaked fish, chives, veggies, egg and cheese.

5. Leave to cool. After a while, make the mixture into balls (each ball should be about the size of a golf ball). Form the balls into a croquette (you can store by arranging balls on a foil-lined tray and placing in a refrigerator for about 30 minutes before transferring to a freezer bag. Defrost when you need to cook.

6. To cook directly, place balls on baking tray and place in preheated oven for 15 to 20 minutes till cooked through.

7. Leave to cool completely (especially on the inside) before serving to your baby.

RECIPES FOR DESSERTS AND FAMILY DINNERS

Baby Friendly Turkish Kebabs

Time: 25 minutes | Amount:4 servings (for 2 babies and 2 adults)

Ingredients:

- ♦ Minced beef
- ♦ Grated white onion (1, medium)
- ♦ Crushed garlic (2 cloves)
- ♦ Lemon juice (1/2)
- ♦ Finely chopped fresh parsley (a small bunch)
- ♦ Ground cumin (2 tsp)
- ♦ Ground paprika (2 tsp)
- ♦ Black pepper (to season)
- ♦ Kebab skewers

For Yogurt dressing

- ♦ Greek yogurt (1 cup)
- ♦ Juice (from one lemon)
- ♦ Pepper (to season)

How to prepare:

1. Preheat oven to 400F/180C

2. Add all ingredient for kebab into a bowl & mix well until fully combined.

3. Divide mixture into 10 parts and mould each one into the shape of a long sausage with you hands.

4. Stick skewer into each piece and place on baking tray lined with parchment paper. Kebabs can be stored in a freezable container in a fridge until you are ready to cook.

5. To cook, place baking tray into oven & bake for 10 to 12 minutes. Turn the kebabs over then leave to bake for 10-12 more minutes till cooked through.

6. To prepare yogurt dressing, combine all the Ingredients: for the dressing in a bowl.

7. Kebabs can be served with lettuce, sweet onion or chopped tomato with the sauce drizzled on it.

Apple Pie Chia Pudding

Time:4 minutes | Amount: 4 small puddings

Ingredients:

- Apple puree (1.5 cup)
- Milk (1.5 cup)
- Chia seeds (4 tbsp)
- 1/3 cup apple purée (4oz/100g)
- 2 Tbsp chia seeds
- Cinnamon (1 tsp)
- 1/3 cup milk or milk alternative (approx 80 - 85 ml)
- Cinnamon (1/4 - 1/2 tsp)

How to prepare:

1. Pour all Ingredients: into a bowl.

2. Combine Ingredients: and ensure they are well mixed.

3. Pour Ingredients: into a jar or bowl and refrigerate for 18 to 20 minutes before you serve.

Tandoori Fish Bites

Ingredients:

♦ Paprika (1 tbsp)

♦ Coriander (1/2 tsp)

♦ Nutmeg (1/4 tsp)

♦ Natural yogurt (150ml)

♦ Black pepper

♦ White fish (450g/16oz)

♦ Cumin (1 tsp)

♦ Rapeseed oil

For dipping sauce

♦ Natural yogurt (200ml)

♦ Fresh coriander leaves (small bunch, chopped)

♦ Juice and zest (from half lime)

♦ Cumin (a pinch)

♦ Black pepper

How to prepare:

1. Prepare oven by preheating to about 190C/400F

2. Add the yogurt & spices into a bowl and mix till well combined.

3. Cut fish into bite-sized chunks then place in a bowl along with the other Ingredients:. Mix thoroughly until well coated

4. Add fish mixture into in a parchment sheet-lined baking dish. Spread around to ensure that the pieces are not touching. Drizzle lightly with some rapeseed oil

5. Place tray in prepared oven and bake for 15 to 20 minutes. Drain off excess liquid and cook for 10 additional minutes.

6. To prepare sauce, add yogurt, lime juice, coriander leaves & pepper in a bowl then mix. Top mixture with ground cumin and some more coriander leaves

7. To serve, put fish bites in a serving bowl and add the dressing on top.

Spinach Muffins

Time: 30 minutes | Amount: 12 muffins

Ingredients:

♦ Banana (250g/8g)

♦ Frozen spinach (100g)

♦ Milk (150ml)

♦ Maple syrup (2 tbsp)

♦ 1 egg

♦ Melted butter (50ml)

♦ Rolled oats (1 cup)

♦ Flour (1 cup)

♦ Baking powder (2 tsp)

How to prepare:

1. Put banana, milk and spinach into a blender and blend to form a green smoothie

2. Pour smoothie into a bowl. Add milk and egg then whisk

3. Add the dry ingredient to the egg-milk mixture then mix thoroughly with a wooden spoon.

4. Bake dough formed in an oven for 25 to 30 minutes.

5. Remove from oven and leave to cool before you serve.

6. Muffins can be refrigerated in an airtight jar for up to 3 days.

Cinnamon Roasted Butternut Squash with Cranberries

Time: 35 minutes | Amount:4 servings (2 babies and 2 adults)

Ingredients:

- Butternut squash
- Cinnamon (1 tsp)
- Olive oil (4 tbsp)
- Allspice (1/4 tsp)
- Maple syrup(2 tbsp)
- Finely chopped rosemary (2 sprigs) goat cheese (60g/2oz)
- Fresh cranberries (1 cup)
- Juice (from 1/2 orange
- Fresh parsley (a small bunch)

How to prepare:

1. Preheat oven to 180C/380F

2. Deseed butternut squash and peel then cut into small cubes about 1inch each. Place cubes into a large bowl.

3. Add olive oil, all spice, cinnamon, rosemary & maple syrup then use your hands to mix well until the butternut squash is fully covered.

4. Pour Ingredients: into a parchment paper lined baking tray. Leave to roast in oven for 24 minutes then remove from oven.

5. Add orange juice & cranberries. Toss in sauce using a spatula. Return to oven for another 10 to 15 minutes until the cranberries begin to pot open.

6. Remove from oven & serve with fresh parsley.

3 Minute Strawberry Vegan Ice Cream

Time: 4 minutes | Amount:4 servings

Ingredients:

♦ Frozen strawberries (2 cups)

♦ Cashews (1 cup)

♦ Dates (3)

How to prepare:

1. Put all the Ingredients: into blender/ food processor.

2. Blitz for about 3 minutes. The mixture will have a fine sand texture at first but should turn to a creamy smooth ice-cream as you continue.

3. It is best served immediately but can be frozen for later as well.

Strawberry Chia Yoghurt Parfaits

Time: 7 minutes | Amount: 3 parfaits

Ingredients:

♦ Strawberries (1 cup) (fresh or frozen)

♦ Water (3 tsp)
maple syrup (2 tbsp)

♦ Chia seeds (2 tbsp)

♦ Greek yogurt (1 cup)

How to prepare:

1. Pour strawberries & water into a big pot. Leave to simmer until strawberries are softened. Use a spoon to mash berries.

2. Turn the heat off.

3. Add chia seeds and maple syrup then mix thoroughly then leave to cool

4. Once cooled, layer the strawberry-chia jam and greek yogurt into jars to form parfaits.

Pesto Pasta with Roasted Veggies and Balsamic Tomatoes

Time: 20 minutes | Amount: 4 to 5 servings

Ingredients:

- Water (2 liters)
- Whole wheat pasta (350g/13oz)
- Courgettes (2)
- Red bell peppers (2)
- Olive oil

Pesto

- Pine nuts (100g/4oz)
- Basil leaves (70g/3oz)
- Garlic (2 cloves)
- Backed black pepper
- Balsamic tomatoes
- Balsamic vinegar
- Cherry tomatoes (15 to 16)

How to prepare:

1. Cook pasta in a saucepan based on he instruction on the pack

2. While pasta is cooking, prepare peppers by cutting in half and deseeding then cutting into 8 spears.

3. Drizzle with oil and place the pepper with the skin side up in a grill. Cook for 5 to 7 minutes till the skin begins to char.

4. Flip pepper over & cook for some minutes on the other side.

5. Remove pepper and lay aside in a bowl covered with a cling film.

6. Slice courgette & drizzle with oil. Place courgette under under the grill a swell and cook for about 5 minutes until browned on one side (ensure that the courgette does not get burned).

7. Meanwhile put all the pesto Ingredients: in blender and blend into a smooth and silky sauce.

8. Pour sauce into a pan then place over medium heat. Stir gently as it cooks until fragrant.

9. The pasta should be well-cooked at this point. Drain pasta and add the pesto pan. Mix with the sauce until pasta is fully coated with sauce.

10. Cut cherry tomatoes into 4 pieces each and add to a bowl along with the remining Ingredients:. Mix well then decorate pasta with them.

11. Drizzle with some oil and balsamic mixture

12. Leave to cool then serve

Low-Sugar Reindeer Cookies

Time: 35 minutes | Amount: 24 cookies

Ingredients:

- ♦ Apple puree or apple sauce (1 cup)
- ♦ Chia seeds (1 tbsp)
- ♦ Dates (6)
- ♦ Coconut oil or butter (60g)
- ♦ Vanilla (1 tsp)
- ♦ Flour (2 cups)
- ♦ Cinnamon (1 tsp)
- ♦ Ground ginger (1 to 2 tsp)
- ♦ Ground almonds (1 cup)
- ♦ Baking powder (1 tsp)
- ♦ White icing

How to prepare:

1. Add chia seeds to apple sauce then leave to sit in for about 20 minutes.

2. Add in dates, vanilla and melted butter then pour all into a food processor. Blitz well until a smooth paste is formed.

3. Add dry Ingredients: (flour, ground almond, baking powder, cinnamon, ginger and mixed spice) into a bowl. Mix well using a fork until well combined

4. Add wet Ingredients: from food processor into bowl of dry Ingredients:. Mix well to form dough using a wooden spoon.

5. Turn dough onto a smooth board or countertop and knead till a smooth dough is formed.

6. Roll out dough to a thickness of 5mm then cut into desired shape.

7. Place cookies on a parchment paper-lined tray and place in oven.

8. Bake for 15 to 24 minutes.

9. Remove from oven, leave to cool and decorate with icing then serve.

Halloween Garlic Mushroom Skulls

Time: 30 minutes | Amount:4 servings (2 adults and 2 kids)

Ingredients:

♦ Mushrooms (8)

♦ Garlic (4 cloves, crushed)

♦ Juice (from 1/2 lemon)

♦ Pepper (added to season)

♦ Breadcrumbs (2 cups)

♦ Garlic (2 cloves (crushed) to breadcrumbs)

♦ Fresh parsley (1 handful, finely chopped)

♦ Rapeseed oil (1 tbsp)

How to prepare:

1. Prepare oven by preheating to 350F/180C

2. Carve out mushroom skulls by carving 2 triangles for the eyes and 1 for a mouth.

3. Place skulls on a baking tray with flat side down. Add lemon juice, crushed garlic, and oil then season with pepper. Rub in the oil and lemon mixture with your fingers,

4. In another baking tray, mix breadcrumbs with crushed garlic, oil and parley then stir well with a spoon.

5. Place mushroom in the oven and bake for 18 to 20 minutes. Also, bake bread-crumbs for about 14 minutes until crispy (not browned)

6. Spoon breadcrumbs into a bowl and add a skewer into the mushroom head and place on breadcrumbs. Spoon some juice from mushroom over it.

7. To be served warm

WEEKLY MEAL PLANNER

DAY 1

Breakfast: *Easy Cheesy Blender Scrambled Eggs*

(Serves 2/6minutes)

Ingredients:

- 3 eggs
- Milk (1/4 cup)
- Cheddar cheese (30g/1oz)
- Oil or butter for greasing pan

Directions:

1. Pour eggs, cheese and milk into a blender and blitz
2. Pour mixture into well-greased non-stick pan
3. Move the egg mixture around the pan slowly using a wooden spoon
4. Cook until soft consistency is achieved
5. Serve with fresh bread

Lunch: *Baby Friendly Turkish Kebabs p-77*
Dinner: *Finger Fish Fruit Cakes p-62*

DAY 2

Breakfast: *Sweet Potato Wedges p-16*

Lunch: **Tomato Bacon Pasta with Hidden Mushrooms**

(serves: 4/15mins)

Ingredients:

♦ Tomato (1 400g/14oz tin)
♦ Mushrooms (100g/4oz)
♦ Mixed herbs (1/2 tsp)
♦ Oil (1 tbsp)
♦ Streaky bacon (3)
♦ Pasta (300g/11oz)

Directions:

1. Heat pan and add oil then pour in onion slices and bacon. Cook onions and bacon for about 5 minutes.

2. While cooking, add the remaining ingredient into a food processor/blender and blitz shortly.

3. Pour Ingredients: into pan and cook with the onion and bacon

4. Simmer with the pot covered to thicken sauce

5. Stir in cooked pasta and mix

6. Remove from the heat & serve warm.

Dinner: *Fish Pie Bites p-74*

DAY 3

Breakfast: *Baked Apple Slices p-17*

Lunch: *Lentil & Sweet Potato Croquettes p-33*

Dinner: **Sticky Chicken & Veggies Tray Bake**

(Serves 5/50 minutes)

Ingredients:

- Sweet potatoes (4, small)
- Chicken breasts (4)
- Sweet pepper (4, baby sized or 2 regular size)
- Red onions (2)
- White onion (1)
- Garlic (1 bulb)
- Tomatoes (8, baby sized)

For sauce

- Fresh coriander (a small bunch)
- Olive oil (3 tbsp)
- Peaches (2 ripe)
- Dijon mustard (1 tsp)
- Maple syrup(2 tbsp)
- Fresh rosemary
- Ground black pepper

Directions:

1. Preheat oven to 380F/180C
2. Prepare baking tray by lining with parchment paper
3. Chop chicken breasts into bite sized pieces and add to baking tray.
4. Peel sweet potatoes and slice into thick chop, chop sweet pepper in half and remove seeds. Also peel and chop onion into quarters. Add all to the baking tray along with chicken breasts.
5. Remove lose skin around each garlic clove & add to the pan without peeling.
6. To prepare sauce, separate leaves from coriander then set aside (to be used as decoration after dish is cooked).
7. Place coriander sauce along with the rest of the Ingredients: for sauce in a blender and blitz till creamy and smooth.
8. Pour sauce over chicken and vegetables & mix with your hands until thoroughly coated
9. Scatter baby tomatoes over mix then place tray in the oven to bake. Cook for 40 to 45 minutes till vegetables are squishy and soft and chicken is soft and moist.
10. Decorate with roughly-chopped coriander leaves

DAY 4

Breakfast: *Zucchini Banana Bread*

(1 loaf/50 minutes)

Ingredients:

- Standard flour (1 cup)
- Oats (1 cup)
- Brown sugar (1/4 cup)
- Baking powder (1.5 tsp)
- Grated Zucchini (200g/7oz)
- Mashed banana (2 medium)
- Eggs
- Unsweetened yogurt (150g/5oz)
- Blueberries (1 cup)

Directions:

1. Place dry Ingredients: in a large bowl then mix well with a fork or spoon till evenly dispersed.

2. Squeeze grated zucchini to remove all the liquid from it

3. Add zucchini, eggs, banana, and yogurt to dry Ingredients: then mix thoroughly.

4. Pour Ingredients: into a greased and lined bread loaf tin

5. Place the unused blueberries on top of the dough

6. Put loaf tin in oven and bake for about 45 to 50 minutes until it turns a golden brown color.

7. Set aside for 10 minutes to cool in the tin then remove, slice and serve when cooled.

Lunch: *Salmon Sweet Potato Fritters p-35*
Dinner: *Potato Salad p-68*

DAY 5

Breakfast: Baby Apple and Oats Pancakes p-28

Lunch: **Mini Toast Burgers**

(1 burger/3mins)

Ingredients:

♦ Toast (2 slices)
♦ Cooked burger patty (1)
♦ Salads

Directions:

1. Cut a desired sized circle from each toast slice using a cookie cutter or glass
2. Shape the cooked burger patty into desired sized using the cookie cutter
3. Assemble burger with the salad as filling and serve.

Dinner: Chicken Meatballs p-73

DAY 6

Breakfast: *Avocado Toasts p-20*

Lunch: *Vegetable Quinoa Biscuits p-37*

Dinner: **Lamb and Butternut Squash Tagine**

(16 baby portions/2 hrs 20mins)

Ingredients:

- Lean lamb (diced, 400g/14oz)
- Plain flour (1 tbsp)
- White onions (2 small, finely diced)
- Crushed garlic (4 cloves)
- Tomato puree (2 tbsp, unsalted)
- Dried cumin (3 tsp)
- Olive oil (2 tbsp)
- Dried coriander (3 tsp)
- Dried tumeric (1 tsp)
- 1 Butternut squash (medium)
- Home made stock or water (750ml)
- Cinnamon (1 stick)
- Chopped tomatoes (1 tin)
- Ground black pepper (1/2 tsp)
- Medjool dates (6 pitted)

Directions:

1. Preheat oven to 180C/380F

2. Cut diced lamb again if too big for baby

3. Heat oil in a pan or skillet and pour in onions to fry for 5 to 8 minutes until caramelized.

4. Add small pieces of the lamb & cook for 2-3 minues till it starts to turn brown (do not overcook).

5. Add in flour and stir-cook for about 30 seconds to thicken the sauce

6. Add tomato puree and stir further until all Ingredients: in the pot are well combined

7. Transfer mixture into an oven-ready dish and cover with a lid or tin foil.

8. Bake for 2 hours on medium heat. You may also use a slow cooker (4 to 6 hrs in slow cooker on medium heat).

9. Take the lid off the dish for the last 20 minutes of cooking. This will help thicken the sauce.

10. Remove from oven. Can be served with home-made bread.

DAY 7

Breakfast: Blueberry Banana Baked Breakfast Oats

(Serves 8/25mins)

Ingredients:

- Bananas (2, medium)
- Quick-cook porridge oats (2 cups)
- Milk (2 cups)
- 2 eggs
- Maple syrup (2 tbsp)
- Vanilla (1 tsp)
- Cinnamon (1 tsp)
- Blueberries (1 cup)

Directions:

1. Preheat oven to 360oF/180oC
2. Grease or spray baking dish with oil or butter
3. Slice banana and lay slices at the bottom of your dish
4. Cover banana slices with oats
5. Whisk egg, milk, vanilla, cinnamon and maple syrup.
6. Pour mixed Ingredients: over oats & catter the blueberries on top
7. Place on hot oven then bake for about 25 minutes. Oats should have absorbed liquid by now
8. Serve alone or with milk.

Lunch: Sweet Corn and Spinach Fritters p-30
Dinner: Slow Cooker Chickpea Sweet Potato Korma p-57

Disclaimer

The opinions and ideas of the author contained in this publication are designed to educate the reader in an informative and helpful manner. While we accept that the instructions will not suit every reader, it is only to be expected that the recipes might not gel with everyone. Use the book responsibly and at your own risk. This work with all its contents, does not guarantee correctness, completion, quality or correctness of the provided information. Always check with your medical practitioner should you be unsure whether to follow a low carb eating plan. Misinformation or misprints cannot be completely eliminated. Human error is real!

Designer: Oliviadesign

Picture: pikselstock // shutterstock.com

Printed in Great Britain
by Amazon

40039170R00066